About the Author™

Meet
Cynthia Rylant

Frances E. Ruffin

The Rosen Publishing Group's
PowerKids Press™
New York

For my niece Elizabeth Marie

Published in 2006 by The Rosen Publishing Group, Inc.
29 East 21st Street, New York, NY 10010

Editor: Rachel O'Connor
Layout Design: Julio A. Gil
Photo Researcher: Cindy Reiman

Photo Credits: Cover, pp. 1, 4, 20 courtesy of Cynthia Rylant and Writer's House LLC; p. 7 courtesy West Virginia Division of Tourism; p. 8 George Bragg Collection; pp.10, 11, 17 © Getty Images; p. 12 © Royalty-Free/Corbis; p. 15 Photo of Morris Harvey College (now University of Charleston) courtesy of Morris Harvey Archives. Cynthia Rylant Display courtesy University of Charleston; p. 16 Cabell County Public Library Collection; p. 19 Nicole DiMella; p. 22 Reprinted with permission of Simon & Schuster Children's Publishing Division from a publicity photograph of Cynthia Rylant.

Grateful acknowledgment is made for permission to reprint previously published material:
p. 5 From MISSING MAY by Cynthia Rylant. Published by Dell Publishing, a division of Random House, Inc.
p. 7 From WHEN I WAS YOUNG IN THE MOUNTAINS by Cynthia Rylant, illustrated by Diane Goode. Text copyright © 1982 by Cynthia Rylant. Illustrations © 1982 by Diane Goode. Used by permission of Dutton Children's Books, A Division of Penguin Young Readers Group, A Member of Penguin Group (USA) Inc., 345 Hudson Street, New York, NY 10014. All rights reserved.
p. 13 Excerpt and book cover from THE VAN GOGH CAFE, copyright © 1995 by Cynthia Rylant, reprinted by permission of Harcourt, Inc.
p. 14 Reprinted with the permission of Atheneum Books for Young Readers, an imprint of Simon & Schuster Children's Publishing Division from THE RELATIVES CAME by Cynthia Rylant. Copyright © 1985 Cynthia Rylant.
p. 18 Jacket Cover from MISSING MAY by Cynthia Rylant, copyright © 1992 by Cynthia Rylant. Used by permission of Dell Publishing, a division of Random House, Inc.
p. 21 Reprinted with the permission of Atheneum Books for Young Readers, an imprint of Simon & Schuster Children's Publishing Division from HENRY AND MUDGE: THE FIRST BOOK by Cynthia Rylant, pictures by Sucie Stevenson. Illustrations copyright © 1987 Sucie Stevenson.

Library of Congress Cataloging-in-Publication Data

Ruffin, Frances E.
  Meet Cynthia Rylant / Frances E. Ruffin.— 1st ed.
      p. cm. — (About the author)
  Includes index.
  ISBN 1-4042-3131-5 (library binding)
  1. Rylant, Cynthia—Juvenile literature. 2. Authors, American—20th century—Biography—Juvenile literature. 3. Children's literature—Authorship—Juvenile literature. I. Title. II. Series.
  PS3568.Y55Z87 2006
  813'.54—dc22

                                           2004028299

Manufactured in the United States of America

Contents

Cynthia has always loved dogs. She wrote about a big, friendly dog called Mudge in over 20 books in the Henry and Mudge series. She also wrote about dogs, and where they go after they die, in her book called Dog Heaven.

The Writer from West Virginia

Cynthia Rylant's stories are about the lives of ordinary people. She writes about family reunions, **adventurous** animals, childhood and teenage crushes, the power of **religion**, and the death of loved ones. Many of her stories take place in the mountains of West Virginia, where she grew up.

The town where she lived was small and did not have a public library. Cynthia did not go into a public library until she was in her twenties! It was while she worked in a library at the age of 23 that she discovered all the wonderful children's books she had not read as a child. These books **inspired** her to write her own stories for children.

"May was the best person I ever knew. Even better than Ob. She was a big barrel of nothing but love, and while Ob and me were off in our dreamy heads, May was here in this trailer seeing to it there was a good home for us when we were ready to land."

—From p. 15, Missing May

A Family Separation

Cynthia was born on June 6, 1954, in Hopewell, Virginia. She was the only child of John Tune and Leatrel Rylant Smith. Her parents separated when she was four. Cynthia went to live with her grandparents, who lived in a mining town in the **Appalachian Mountains** of West Virginia. Cynthia's mother left her for nearly four years to go to nursing school. While they were apart, Cynthia saw her mother a few times a year. She never saw or heard from her father until, at the age of 13, she began receiving letters from him. He had been living in Florida, and he said he wanted to see her. Soon after Cynthia heard from him, however, her father died.

Here is a view of the Appalachian Mountains near where Cynthia grew up. Her book *When I Was Young in the Mountains* ends with the words, "I never wanted to go anywhere else in the world, for I was in the mountains. And that was always enough."

Cool Ridge was the coal-mining town where Cynthia lived with her grandparents. Her grandfather worked in a coal mine, like the one shown here, until he was hurt and could not work anymore.

A Childhood in the Mountains

Cynthia's grandparents lived in Cool Ridge, West Virginia. Two uncles, two aunts, and two cousins also lived with them. It was cozy in their little white house. However, the house had no electricity, no running water, and no indoor toilets. All the water used for cooking and washing dishes and clothes had to be brought from a well near the house. Once a week Cynthia's grandmother heated up a big metal tub of water for baths. Although Cynthia later realized they had been poor, she had never lacked for love there. She says that it was the gentle strength of her loving grandparents that helped her **survive** being left by her parents.

Cynthia's uncle Joe was her hero. He was good looking and was a great basketball player. When Cynthia was 12, Uncle Joe fought in the Vietnam War. In her book Blue-Eyed Daisy, Cynthia wrote about an uncle who was a soldier and a hero.

Like the girls in the picture here, Cynthia and her friends were crazy about the Beatles. Cynthia stood in line for two hours when the Beatles' first movie, A Hard Day's Night, *came to theaters. She was 10 years old at the time, and she remembers yelling and crying with the rest of the audience.*

My Adventures with the Beatles

Cynthia was eight when she left her grandparents' home. Her mother had become a nurse and had found an apartment in the nearby town of Beaver, West Virginia. The apartment was in one half of a house. In the other half lived a boy, Ronnie, who became Cynthia's longtime childhood friend.

In 1964, when Cynthia was 10, the Beatles, the English rock group, came to America. Cynthia had a crush on the whole band, but she especially liked Paul McCartney. She wore Beatles clothes and necklaces. Cynthia did not write much as a child, but she did write a collection of short stories called *My Adventures with the Beatles* when she was in sixth grade.

Here you can see the Beatles at the start of their American tour in 1964. From left to right are George Harrison, John Lennon, Ringo Starr, and Paul McCartney. Cynthia kept a picture of Paul McCartney beside her bed and had posters of him on her walls. In some ways Paul McCartney was a male role model for her. She looked up to him.

When Cynthia was in junior high, the New Orleans Symphony Orchestra came to play at her school in Beaver. An orchestra is a group of people who play music together. Seeing the conductor and his orchestra helped Cynthia realize there was a world outside of Beaver. It was a world she wanted to discover.

Growing Up in Beaver

Cynthia's mother could not provide for many **luxuries** on her nurse's salary. Their home had no rugs. Their front yard had a view of a junkyard. Cynthia worried that one day the apartment's old gas heaters would blow up the house. She longed to live in the kind of houses that she saw in magazines. Cynthia thought that one classmate, Christy Sanders, had the ideal home. She imagined the furniture matched, and the house smelled of chocolate-marshmallow cookies. She wanted to live in a house like Christy's. She felt that the town of Beaver was dull and poor. There were no libraries or art museums there. Cynthia knew she wanted a life outside Beaver. She wanted more than she had.

"And as he sits, the magic in those walls begins its work on him. There in the Van Gogh Cafe, he is reminded of what he is and what he finds beautiful."

—From pp. 52–53, The Van Gogh Cafe

13

Life and Education

Cynthia's father had served in the **Korean War**. This gave Cynthia the opportunity to go to college on a **scholarship** for the children of men who had been in the military. In 1975, she earned a Bachelor of Arts **degree** in English from Morris Harvey College in West Virginia. English was a required subject for first-year students. Cynthia discovered she liked it. She went on to get a Master of Arts degree in English from Marshall University in West Virginia. In 1982, she received a Master of Library Science degree from Kent State University in Ohio. During her years at university, Cynthia married and **divorced** twice. She gave birth to her only child, Nate, in 1978.

Cynthia earned her bachelor's degree in English at Morris Harvey College in West Virginia. It is now called the University of Charleston. Inset: The university has set up a special display, which features a picture of Cynthia, along with some of her books.

When Cynthia worked at the Cabell County Public Library, shown here, she was surrounded by children's books, and she read as many as she could.

Cynthia the Librarian

After graduating from Morris Harvey College, 23-year-old Cynthia found a job at the Cabell County Public Library in Huntington, West Virginia. She was assigned to work in the children's room. While working there she discovered children's **literature**. She read books such as *Make Way for Ducklings* and *Ox-Cart Man*. These were books she had not read during her own childhood. Without a library nearby, Cynthia had grown up reading Nancy Drew **novels** from the local store.

The books that now surrounded her at her library job inspired her to write her own stories. When she felt they were good enough, she mailed some of these stories out to book **publishers**.

Among the writers who inspired Cynthia to write was poet Randall Jarrell, shown here. Mr. Jarrell wrote a children's book called The Animal Family. Cynthia said this was the book that made her want to write. As well as writing children's books, Cynthia also writes poetry. Her books of poetry include Waiting to Waltz: A Childhood *and* Soda Jerk.

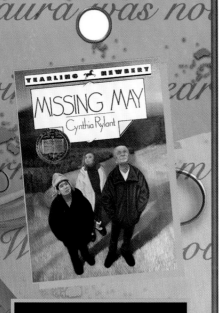

In 1993, Cynthia's book Missing May won the Newbery Medal for the most distinguished novel for children published that year. Missing May tells how Summer, a 12-year-old girl, searches for the strength to go on living after the sudden death of a much-loved aunt.

Writing from Memories

In 1982, when she was 25, Cynthia's first book *When I Was Young in the Mountains* was published. She **dedicated** the book to her grandparents. It was based on her memories of their home in the mountains and of the four years that she lived with them. In 1983, Cynthia and the book's **illustrator**, Diane Goode, won a Caldecott Honor. This is an **award** given each year by the American Library Association (ALA) for the most **distinguished** picture book. In 1986, Cynthia and illustrator Stephen Gammell won a Caldecott Honor for her book *The Relatives Came*. This is a story about a country family reunion. It was also based on her memories of her grandparents' Appalachian home.

When I Was Young in the Mountains follows the day-to-day life of a young girl living in the mountains in West Virginia. As well as winning a Caldecott Honor, the book also received the American Book Award in 1982.

Cynthia has also illustrated some of her books. The first book she illustrated was her book for young readers Dog Heaven, which was published in 1995. Cat Heaven and Give Me Grace are other books that Cynthia has illustrated.

Happy at Last

Cynthia had a hard childhood. She grew up without a father and was separated from her mother. Yet Cynthia has found happiness as an adult. Today Cynthia lives in Washington State. She loves being a writer. For Cynthia being a writer makes her feel free. She can write whatever she wants, whenever she wants. She has said that being a writer lets her leave something here on Earth. In an **interview** Cynthia said, "I want to do something important in my life, and I think that adding beauty to the world with books like *The Relatives Came*, *Waiting to Waltz*, or *Henry and Mudge and the Forever Sea* really is important."

One of Cynthia's husbands owned a large dog from which Cynthia created the character of Mudge. Mudge is the big, lovable dog that often gets into trouble in her Henry and Mudge books. Cynthia based the character of Henry on her son, Nate. In real life Nate was often caught up in the kinds of adventures found in the Henry and Mudge series.

21

In Her Own Words

Why do you write children's books?

I love children's books. . . . There was something about children's literature that flooded me with **exhilaration**. . . . I'm not interested in trying to entertain only children. If they like the books, that's fine, but I really expect everybody to like them.

So you don't write with a specific age group in mind?

No. Not at all.

What is your work routine?

The picture books I write in about an hour. . . . I'll write maybe two or three of those in a year. Some years I've written as many as five picture books. That's about five hours' work out of 365 days. And then they become great, wonderful, forever books. With the novels, I make a decision that I will write a novel and I make a decision about which season I'll start [the novel].

What sort of advice do you give to beginning children's book writers?

To write as many books as you can. You have to write 20 the first year you try. Out of the 20, maybe one of them is really good, and if it is, I truly believe it will be purchased [by a publisher]. And to, of course, set the highest standards possible . . . and remember what really fine literature sounds like. And don't settle for anything less.

Glossary

adventurous (ed-VEN-cheh-rus) Doing new and exciting things, bold.

Appalachian Mountains (a-puh-LAY-chun MOWN-tenz) A mountain chain in the eastern part of the United States.

award (uh-WORD) Something that is given after careful thought.

dedicated (DEH-dih-kayt-ed) Gave to a purpose.

degree (dih-GREE) A title given to a person who has finished a course of study.

distinguished (dih-STING-wishd) Something that is outstanding.

divorced (dih-VORSD) Ended a marriage legally.

exhilaration (ig-zih-luh-RAY-shun) A feeling of great delight.

illustrator (IH-lus-tray-ter) A person who draws or paints pictures that go with a story.

inspired (in-SPYRD) Filled with excitement about something.

interview (IN-ter-vyoo) When someone questions someone else.

Korean War (kuh-REE-un WOR) The war fought by North Korea against South Korea from 1950 to 1953.

literature (LIH-tuh-ruh-chur) Writings such as books, plays, and poetry.

luxuries (LUK-shuh-reez) Comforts and beauties of life that are not necessary.

novels (NAH-vulz) Long stories about made-up people and events.

publishers (PUH-blih-shurz) Companies whose business is printing and selling books, newspapers, or magazines.

religion (rih-LIH-jen) A belief in and a way of honoring a god or gods.

scholarship (SKAH-ler-ship) Money given to someone to pay for school.

survive (sur-VYV) To continue to exist.

Index

Web Sites

Due to the changing nature of Internet links, PowerKids Press has developed an online list of Web sites related to the subject of this book. This site is updated regularly. Please use this link to access the list: www.powerkidslinks.com/aa/cynrylant/